T0163741

Estimated Time of Departure

ADVANCE PRAISE

Decades of empirical research have documented the transformative and educational power of narrative. Reading stories about others' experiences can provide deep insight into one's own life, it can bring people together by illuminating what may otherwise feel as an isolating experience, and it can normalize some of the seemingly arduous aspects of life. Nowhere can this be seen as vividly as in stories surrounding the process of traversing end of life discussions and experiences. In *Estimated Time of Departure* William Donaldson expertly creates a sense of intimacy by bringing us into his world. His narrative is engaging and often humorous as he tells the stories of his family's end of life discussions. In doing so, he makes the reader feel like a friend along for the ride. Interwoven with his experiences are concrete suggestions for the reader to consider in thinking about their own stories and how they may have end of life conversations with their parents, children, or even with themselves. Given the importance of these conversations, and the rarity with which they occur, *Estimated Time of Departure* is significant insofar as it shows us a roadmap for how to engage in what can seem like a daunting task: confronting the end of one's story on earth. By showing how transformative end of life discussions can be, Donaldson not only shares his own experiences but also encourages us to craft our own stories. Without being pedantic or heavy handed, Donaldson gently guides us through the process in hopes of helping others achieve what scholars have dubbed "a good death." Health educators and hospice workers have long known the importance of striving to end life on one's own terms. Similarly, communication experts have long exalted the importance of discussing end of life decisions with our loved ones. Here, Donaldson provides specific questions we should engage with and offers prompts for topics to discuss. The narrative he presents is insightful, realistic, relatable, and makes the difficult to tackle just a little bit easier. An enjoyable and insightful read, *Estimated Time of Departure* allows the reader to harness the power of narrative to navigate their own end of life stories and hopefully helps others to achieve the good death that Donaldson was able to facilitate for his family.

Dr. Alice Veksler,
Specialist in Medical Communications

In times that feel increasingly uncertain, there is something we can all do to give ourselves ultimate peace of mind, and that is to contemplate and make important decisions regarding the one thing sure to happen eventually: our death, and the death of those we love. Facing death in a death-phobic culture is a task few people undertake on purpose. Willy Donaldson has done so and, with grace and a vital sense of warmth and humor, inspires us to do the same.

After navigating the many complexities surrounding his own father's and mother's departures, Willy generously offers up the wisdom he gleaned from his personal experience, as a blueprint for untangling the knotted path that lies at the end of everyone's life.

How we navigate this path is important, for individuals, their families, and communities, as well as for culture and for humanity. It matters how the story ends. What does dying well look like, considering one's core values? Willy invites us into a safe space to ask this question of ourselves and our loved ones. He serves as a practical example of how to go about the tender, trying business of dying a human death, and shows us how we can prepare for our own like we would for any other sacred human experience that requires an alchemic combination of preparation, adaptability, and surrender.

Anna Marshall,
End of Life Caregiver, Death Doula

Willy Donaldson's poignant memoir *Estimated Time of Departure* provides a refreshingly direct yet gentle perspective on relationships in the last phase of life. He reminds us of that most special opportunity we have as children of aging parents to serve as loving advocates and stewards of lives well-lived. If we are aging parents, he teaches us about letting go and how to accept the care and support we deserve. As a social work educator with a background in caregiving relationships, what I found the most surprising and valuable was the thread of hope he weaves throughout his journey. By illuminating the myriad of pathways down which we can walk (and talk) with our loved ones in their final years, months, and days, he provides us with hope that there isn't just one perfect way to do this...that with persistent yet tender communication, it is possible the end of life, while difficult, will be innately rewarding and intimate.

Diane Griffiths, PhD

How I Talked My Parents to Death.

A Love Story.

ESTIMATED TIME of
DEPARTURE

WILLIAM DONALDSON

AITIA PRESS NEW YORK

Estimated Time of Departure

How I Talked My Parents to Death
A Love Story

© 2022 William Donaldson

Published in New York, New York, by Aitia Press, an imprint of Morgan James Publishing. Morgan James is a trademark of Morgan James, LLC. www.AitiaPress.com

Proudly distributed by Ingram Publisher Services.

Morgan James
BOGO™

A **FREE** ebook edition is available for you
or a friend with the purchase of this print book.

CLEARLY SIGN YOUR NAME ABOVE

Instructions to claim your free ebook edition:
1. Visit MorganJamesBOGO.com
2. Sign your name CLEARLY in the space above
3. Complete the form and submit a photo of this entire page
4. You or your friend can download the ebook to your preferred device

ISBN 9781631957116 paperback
ISBN 9781631957123 ebook
Library of Congress Control Number:
20211913458

Cover Design by:
Mitch Phillips
www.designedbymitch.com

Interior Design by:
Christopher Kirk
www.GFSstudio.com

Morgan James is a proud partner of Habitat for Humanity Peninsula and Greater Williamsburg. Partners in building since 2006.

Get involved today! Visit MorganJamesPublishing.com/giving-back

DEDICATION

This book is dedicated to all the nurses, social workers, hospice staff, doctors, death doulas, activists, family members, and others who are trying to change the way we think about end-of life and prepare people for a good death.

We all owe life a death, an inevitable death which we can meet.
— Laura Bohannan

TABLE OF CONTENTS

ACKNOWLEDGMENTS

First and foremost, I must acknowledge my parents. They supported and encouraged me, asked me to help them, and let me go on their journey with them. They were the inspiration for this book and for so much else good in my life.

My sister and brothers who went on the journey with me and who have given me so much over the years. I have cried and laughed with them and succeeded and failed with them. They have carried me, and I have carried them.

The fabulous Marshall sisters. My publisher Bethany Marshall has believed in me and this story. Her support and vision have carried it to completion. I cannot thank her enough.

Bethany introduced me to Anna, an end-of-life care giver and death doula, and she has become an inspirational co-traveler in this journey.

The wonderful gang at Morgan James Publishing once again enveloped me in their nurturing arms and helped us all tell this story.

As with my first book, my editor, Amanda Rooker of SplitSeed, has been invaluable. My graphics muse and social media tour guide, Mitch Phillips, owner of DesignedbyMitch, once again has worked his magic on the cover, the interior concepts, and social media presence. My friend Jesse Hutcheson provided the beautiful photograph of me looking at a picture of my parents on their wedding day.

Colleagues including Alice Veksler, Dianne Griffin, Sherman Lee, Betsy Jelinek, Nathan Harter, Izzy Danstrom, and others provided context and moral support.

INTRODUCTION

Our greatest prejudice is against death.
It spans age, gender, and race. We
spend immeasurable amounts of energy
fighting an event that will eventually
triumph. Though it is noble not to give
in easily, the most alive people I've ever
met are those who embrace their death.
They love, laugh, and live more fully.
— Andy Webster, hospice chaplain

Estimated Time of Departure tells the story of how my experiences of talking with my parents through their end-of-life preparations and ultimate passing turned out to be a celebration of life and love. I found Andy

Webster's words to be true. Far from avoiding these discussions, my family and I leaned into them, and the joy, love, and certainty that came with them were a true gift. My family and I were extraordinarily lucky to have had the time and means to have these important discussions. Importantly, we also took the time to have them.

In *Estimated Time of Departure*, I share my story of these discussions with all the poignancy, love, frustration, laughter, and grace that accompanied them, and I make an impassioned plea for you to have these discussions with your loved ones, be they children, parents or just friends. Please, do not miss this opportunity, for once your loved ones are gone, it is impossible to have these crucial talks.

As you read through *Estimated Time of Departure*, I hope you will see yourself, your family, and your opportunities to gain a deeper understanding of and appreciation for these critical discussions. I hope it will give you the courage to approach these discussions, knowing that they are not just sad and legalistic but joyful and profoundly liberating.

Estimated Time of Departure tells the story of my family's discussions and decisions. This book is not a prescription or roadmap, it is a testament to love and compassion. Your journey, and those of your loved ones, will be different than mine and my family's. Your decisions may be quite different.

I am a businessman, professor, author, and engineer, so I have absolutely no qualifications for offering you medical or estate advice. But I am also a son, brother, father, and life-long learner who learned how powerful and cathartic these seemingly impossible and unpleasant discussions could be. In the decade since I walked this path with my parents, I have researched end-of-life practices, talked with dozens of doctors, nurses, death doulas, hospice workers, administrators, families, and friends. All have implored me to tell this story and share my experience, so I have. I would love to help you find the courage to have these discussions with your loved ones and experience the calm, certainty, and joy that comes with them. Echoing what Andy Webster said, I encourage you to love, laugh, and live more fully.

CHAPTER 1
THE DEPARTURE LOUNGE

Begin with the end in mind.
— Stephen Covey

From an early age, my dad was fascinated by airplanes and flying. At the age of eight, he was determined to build a scale replica of a plane cockpit atop my grandparents' garage. Thinking a child would never complete such a feat, my grandfather, one of the earliest naval aviators, encouraged his hopeful aviator-in-training to attempt the feat. My grandfather later told me it was with great pride and no small measure of irritation that he witnessed my dad complete his project. Granddad allowed that while the model was meticulous, accurate,

1

and skillfully executed, the creation was quite unsightly on the roof of the garage, and some neighbors were not the least bit amused by its looming presence.

Dad continued to explore all manner of things, learning carpentry, foundry, black-smithing, and many other skills. His interest in how things worked, matched with his passion for aviation, eventually led him to a career in aeronautical engineering. He became a pilot, a noted aeronautical engineer, and a fluid phys-icist. His professional work immersed him deeply in war efforts at the National Advisory Committee on Aeronautics (the forerunner of NASA) at the dawn of jet aircraft and, eventu-ally, the space program.

Dad had a powerful intellect—I believe he still holds the record for getting his PhD in the shortest time from his alma mater—and yet he had a kind demeanor and an artistic sense. He taught himself to paint, to build and restore furniture, and to play the guitar and piano. He loved to dance and listen to music, especially jazz. With a deep love for this country, he served it during World War II and on numerous boards and government panels, including the Naval Research Advisory Committee (NRAC), the President's Air Quality Board, and the Marine Corps panel of the NRAC, among others. For his contributions to the field of aeronautics and engineering, he was inducted into the National Academy of Engineering in 1979. He was my hero, my muse, my friend, and my dad but a tough nut to crack and a hard act to follow.

My mom was a self-described tomboy as a youth who loved to skip stones and school. Apparently, she was an accomplished actress as well as she claimed to be able to con her mother into letting her miss school with the mere act of sniffling and looking pathetic. Despite her penchant for skipping school, she read voraciously and explored deeply. Her father, who owned a metal foundry, saw to it that all his girls were educated and had useful skills. Mom went to junior college and learned typing and business skills. Her early athleticism stayed with her, and she went on to excel in golf and tennis socially. Her father was most proud of the fact that he never laid anyone off during the Great Depression. He treated his workers like family. I believe this trait rubbed off on my mom. She had three sisters, lived through the Depression, and was fiercely protective of her family.

Mom grew up to be opinionated and passionately independent. Keenly interested in others, she could carry on a conversation with anyone and be funny and engaging. Fascinated by our planet, she showed an early interest in ecology. She was a marvel and an enigma who could swear, work, drink, and argue with any man but then switch to heels and dance the night away. She brooked no nonsense and could be a stern disciplinarian. A nurse she was not. Her idea of medical intervention was limited to aspirin for pain, vigorous scrubbing for wounds, and honey, whiskey, and lemon (heavy on the whiskey) for a cold, all administered with a healthy dose of stoicism and without a hint of practiced bedside manner.

Through good times and bad, this unlikely pair lived, loved, and raised a family I am proud to be part of. My flights with them and my siblings were not without turbulence, but we all made it to our destinations. My siblings and I could not go on our parents' last trips with them, but we all saw them off in the departure lounge.

Prior to flying, pilots are required to file a flight plan. Wikipedia gives a description of *flight plan*:

> Flight plans are documents filed by a pilot or flight dispatcher with the local Civil Aviation Authority... prior to departure which indicates the plane's planned route or flight path. They generally include basic information such as departure and arrival points, estimated time of departure, estimated time in route, alternate airports in case

of bad weather, type of flight…,
the pilot's information, number of
people on board and information
about the aircraft itself… Flight
plans are highly recommended,
especially when flying over inhos-
pitable areas, such as water, as they
provide a way of alerting rescuers
if the flight is overdue[1].

My dad, being the detail-oriented person
he was, and my mom, being the decisive,
action-oriented person she was, decided they
wanted to have all their affairs in order long
before one or both left the departure lounge on
the exciting flight to the Great Unknown. This
desire saw Dad, Mom, my brother Alec, and I
all pitching in to coordinate the legal house-
keeping. We met in Richmond at an estate
attorney's office to start the process.

With the help of our lawyer, we put
together a will, powers of attorney, durable
medical powers of attorney, and a Do Not

Resuscitate (DNR) order for each parent. We tried to think through all the medical and financial eventualities, taking all the legal and medical steps recommended by the attorneys and our own research. We followed the available checklists to make sure we were thorough. Mom and Dad attended to all details in a workmanlike fashion and with a sense of fatalism that sometimes caught me and my siblings off guard. However, we soldiered on and completed the tasks as they came up.

We did it! We had a solid flight plan, custom made to Dad's and Mom's wishes. We were all set. After signing and distributing all the documents and explaining them to all the parties involved—both family and professionals—we all felt good about where we were.

But as I continued along the journey with my parents, increasingly it felt that something was missing.

I now know that, at the time, we had only dealt with the legal and medical aspects of Mom and Dad's end-of-life journeys. We had done the easy part, the clear part, the non-emotional part.

Don't get me wrong; estate planning is a critical step that many families do not tend to. But I now know that by focusing on the legal issues, we had entirely missed the most important part of the flight plan. You see, we have two tracks to our life: biological and biographical. And we have two minds: rational and emotional. Therefore, there are two stories to tell, *two flight plans to file*. The rational and biological story involves all the medical and legal decisions one must, or should, think through. The emotional and biographical story requires deeply involving those you love in the transition you will all experience. As you will learn, the mind and body's ability to deal with the grief surrounding this transition is profoundly affected by your choices.

Mom and Dad did a great job on the rational and biological stories, and Alec and I helped. But what of the emotional and biographical stories? This is where the journey really starts. In the years that have passed, as I talked with families and medical personnel, I found that we were not unique. In my research and through my many discussions, I found very few families deal with the emotional and biographical aspects of end of life.

According to the AARP, 60 percent of Americans do not have a will or estate plan.[2] Of those that do, virtually none have clear instructions or statements concerning the biographical and emotional aspects of their end of life. According to Reuters, only 37 percent of Americans have any form of advanced medical directives.[3]

According to a survey conducted by the Conversation Project, 92 percent of respondents say that talking to one's loved ones about end-of-life is important, but only 32 percent have actually had any kind of conversation. In the same survey, 95% of Americans say they would be willing to talk about their wishes, and 53% even say they would be relieved to discuss it[4]. A survey by California Healthcare

Foundation found that 60 percent of respondents said that making sure their family was not burdened by tough end-of-life decisions is extremely important, but 56 percent have not communicated their wishes.[5]

Does this strike you as odd? It did me. If you knew you had to learn a language because you were going to move to a foreign country, you would probably start planning and talking to people about that move and the need to speak the language. At the least, you would probably investigate the culture and the community.

If you knew you had to learn probability to keep your job—even though you hated probability—you would probably start planning and talking to people about probability, maybe even take classes or watch videos on the subject.

If you knew a storm was coming and going to hit your house, you would probably start planning, talking to professionals, and preparing.

If you knew these things were inevitable, you would act, prepare, talk about, take lessons, make plans, and discuss options. Most likely, you would talk to your family about the transition and how you and they are feeling about it. In fact, planning is the only rational thing to do. Well, we all know we are going to die, right? So, why don't we act? Why don't we plan? Why don't we talk to family and friends? Why aren't we more proactive?

Because it is not a very pleasant topic. Duh! But here is the inescapable fact of life: it ends. Each and every individual life on planet Earth, all 7.7 billion and counting, will someday end. None of us can do anything about that—no exceptions. It logically follows that since we have over five thousand years of documented, civilized society and sentient thought, we would have adjusted well to death and become comfortable talking about it. But nothing could be further from the truth.

Turns out, even after thousands of years, we are terrible at discussing the inevitable. As the statistics cited above indicate, we avoid these end-of-life discussions. Every day, we lose countless friends and loved ones to sudden deaths, like accidents, disease, and murders. We mourn these losses, but perhaps they are the lucky ones. Their end-of-life decision was made for them.

In contrast, those who enjoy a long life— those traditionally called "lucky"—often traverse an endless path of legal affairs, various doctor's appointments, and hospital stays. We watch in despair and apprehension as they are passed through a legal and medical system that seems to care little for the emotional and biographical stories of its occupants and even less for the affected loved ones.

In the United States alone, the amount of money spent on end-of-life medical care is astronomical. Despite this substantial fortune, the quality of service and care during the end of life appears to be working well emotionally and biographically for few people. In countless discussions with doctors, nurses, hospice workers, and caregivers, I heard the same refrain: "People do not, or will not, have these important end-of-life conversations themselves, so they expect their health care professionals to do it for them." Discussions with parents, children, grandparents, family, and friends offered similar takes, which led me to write this book in hopes that others will have the courage to initiate these important discussions with loved ones while they still can. With so much avoidance of the subject, it is no wonder the research indicates that patients experiencing end-of-life care also experience crushing depression and, no shock, their loved ones do, too.

But why should we fear the inevitable? Why should we avoid talking about death when we would discuss and prepare for any other expected outcome? Do you think avoiding these discussions is going to save you or your loved ones from emotional distress? Do you think putting off these conversations will make the process easier or the answers more apparent? Quite the opposite. The researchers I talked to indicated that having these discussions helps people manage the grief profile better.

One obstacle to talking about the inevitability of death is that no one knows exactly what happens after we die. Even so, can you have a philosophy about death? As it turns out, several highly intelligent people from our past thought you could and perhaps should.

Socrates, the Greek philosopher, hypothesized two possibilities. He posited that death represented a dreamless sleep. That does not sound so bad, and after all, who couldn't use a bit more sleep? He also looked at death as a passage to another life. After you die, he reasoned, you move on to another locale where you can relax and hang out with loved ones and friends who have already passed. How bucolic! No problem there at all. So, what is there to fear?

Epicurus, another Greek philosopher, had another thought. Epicurus believed death is the cessation of sensation. He reasoned that when we are, death is not come, and when death is come, we are not. How simple is that? Easy as pie! Concepts of worry, good, evil, and fear only exist if you are sensate. Since you do not feel when you are dead, do not worry. Nothing can vex you after life, so do not worry. No problems here either!

Do you have a philosophy of death? If so, great. You are way ahead of most people in that regard. If not, why not start developing one? You could use a personal death philosophy to ease your mind and comfort your loved ones. They will remember your words and beliefs once you pass on to your next adventure. Or, as a child, you could ease the mind of a parent who does not want to burden their child with emotional thoughts of loss. Knowing you are prepared might help them prepare. Good starting points for constructing a personal philosophy could be writers whose work moves you, religious scriptures that speak to you, and philosophers, both ancient and modern. Or you could ask folks you know what they think death means. You never know what you might find right in front of you. But to form a cohesive philosophy, you do have to start.

My philosophy on death started to form as I explored my feelings around the topic. The first profound shift was when I first met the coordinator of a local hospice service, who shared with me a powerful perspective on death. She said that most people presume, as I did, that death is the opposite of life. She pointed out that my logic was flawed. Death, she said, is not the opposite of life; it is the opposite of birth. Life is what we do in between birth and death. It sounds a lot like Epicurus and the other philosophers. The opposite of life is nothingness, not having existed. But since we are here, we know that is not the case. If we know we are here and will die, then why not start talking about it? Even though it might be difficult, even painful at times, to discuss death with those closest to you, it can also be a beautiful, poignant, and intimate experience.

The second shift was when I spoke with a colleague, and she told me of an African tradition that buoyed my spirits during the incredibly sad times and continues to comfort me today. In this tradition, the physical passing is but a prelude to death. The final death occurs only when the last person on earth remembers you and speaks your name or tells your story. A powerful philosophy and all the more reason to have the conversations with your loved ones and be able to remember them, thus keeping them close to you even after they are gone.

Estimated Time of Departure is about helping my parents develop that second flight plan, the one that deals with the emotional and biographical—the philosophical—elements of a good death. Let me warn you in advance: it is a high-risk flight plan, but it also has the potential for high reward. In fact, the emotional and biographical flight plan is where all the love and poignancy reside. It may be hard to reveal and untangle, but it is worth it.

My most sincere hope is that this book gives you the courage to have these discussions with your loved ones and develop a flight plan of your own—while you still have time. Whether you are a grandparent, parent, child, or grandchild, I hope you will come to see that having these discussions and helping a loved one pass is not an impossible task to be wished away. Rather, it is a perfectly natural part of life to be embraced.

CHAPTER 2
PREBOARDING

A journey of a thousand miles starts with
a single step . . . the step taken to climb the
ladder which gets you into the airplane.
— Ankala Subbarao

Mom and Dad lived on a large farm to which they had retired. With their independent streaks and work ethic, it was the perfect place for them. They would take turns driving the tractor, pruning trees, cutting grass, and generally enjoying retirement. Dad worked in his shop, repairing things, and restoring furniture. Mom relentlessly beat back nature, and at the end of the day, they would sit on the porch or by the fireplace and read while enjoying the obligatory cocktail. This went on for many years, with all of us siblings travelling for visits and events. But it became increasingly clear to my siblings and me, if not my parents, that they would eventually have a hard time managing a large piece of land and its responsibilities. At this time, we all met in Richmond to talk about the estate.

Eventually, Mom and Dad started thinking about more manageable places to move. They put the farm up for sale and started considering all the potential locations to live out the rest of their lives. They considered locations close to their children. After some soul searching, they settled on my area and decided to relocate there.

This decision provided an interesting symmetry to their lives as they had started their married life together in the community they were returning to. As the preponderance of their friends lived in the area, they felt they would be at home. One day, after a very pleasant lunch, we were driving back to my home. I mentioned that the house directly across from mine was for sale. They took note of its small size, proximity to family, friends, and amenities and decided to make an offer.

Friends were excited for me, exclaiming that I had built-in babysitting. Not so much. With Mom and Dad's legendary independent and stoic streaks, babysitting was not their strong suit. But I told my friends not to worry because Mom and Dad were good at the other things the parents of small children needed: cocktails. Mom and Dad were really good at cocktails.

Once settled in, Mom and Dad continued their independent activities. Dad converted a garage in the back of the new house into a shop and spent almost every day there puttering. Mom became the unofficial groundskeeper for the common area island in our turn-around, pruning and raking. One evening I came home from work to find Mom standing in the bed of her pickup truck using a chain saw and hand saw to prune some of the branches of the trees in the island at the center of our neighborhood circle. Life progressed across the street, and Mom and Dad went on trying to be as independent as possible. However, this independent streak often collided with their age-related realities.

Dad had undergone very extensive surgery on his lower back, and he was increasingly troubled with recurring pain, in addition to extensive osteoarthritis. This made everyday tasks, such as putting on socks, walking, and lifting, problematic and painful. However, due to Dad's fierce independence, I would often find him bent over weeding in the garden or picking up something he should not. Inevitably, he would rise in agony and complain about his back. I would point out that he had chosen to weed, chastise him, and remind him that others could help him, but he insisted on doing these things himself. Stubborn and independent! Have I told you that already?

Precisely because of her independent streak, my mom was not immune to such follies. One night as I drove home, I scanned my parents' front yard and home as I did every night. In the fading light, I was troubled by what I thought was an animal moving on the roof of their house. I parked my car and walked across the street to investigate. As I neared, it was clear there was something moving on the roof. The creature bobbed above the ridge-line, occasionally disappearing on the backside of the roof. I rounded the house to the back yard, and to my great frustration—but not sur-prise—the creature turned out to be my seven-ty-six-year-old mother. Mom had put a ladder up to the roof and was cleaning out the gut-ters. Trying to restrain my incredulity, I asked, "What the h**l are you doing on the roof?" She replied, matter-of-factly, "Cleaning the gut-ters." I believe my somewhat terse reply was, "I can see that, but why are *you* doing that?" Her very glib reply was, "Because they needed it!" I could not argue with her logic, and you have to love her spirit. But at that moment, I wanted to wring her neck.

And so, it went with my parents, my stubborn, independent, funny, loving, and boozy parents. However, after many years, even a small house on a quiet street became too much. It was during this period that I became more aggressive in my questioning about their future. Often these entreaties were deflected, and at times, the exchanges were a little heated. Mom and Dad did not like my probing into their affairs, and they often let me know. As I reflect on these times, I see several reasons for the deflection, which have been confirmed in my discussions with others about this phase of life. First, I think their independence and pride predisposed them to deflection; they were not going to willingly give up that independence. Second, I think they did not want to impose on anyone and feared they would be a burden if they did. Finally, I believe they did not want to face the inevitable.

During this time, I did make one small inroad into the forbidden space. I did get Mom and Dad to have a brief, terse discussion on funeral arrangements. Both were highly dismissive of the whole concept, their general take being that they would be dead and would, therefore, care little about the particulars of their funerals. They both said it was up to me and my siblings, but that did not help. What did they want or not want?

It turns out they were better able to articulate what they *did not* want. They did not want a lot of fuss or high drama. They did not want big, elaborate services, just friends and family for a small memorial. In teasing out some of what they did not want, we made some grudging progress on what they *did* want: songs, readings, etc. Each wanted to be cremated and not buried. As we wound up these discussions, Mom and Dad seemed relieved, but I also sensed they thought we were done. I said that we had a lot more to discuss, and I pointed out that talking about funeral plans was like planning for overtime after you have already lost the game in question. My humor was not appreciated.

And so, it went—thrust, parry, and riposte—like a surreal fencing match. We continued our course, me pushing, and them deflecting. Driving around the circle one afternoon at the end of the day, I saw my mom working in the common area. I stopped to say hello and chat. As we parted, she declared that she and Dad had decided to move to a retirement home. Wow! All those attempted talks and this is the first I heard of it. And so it goes: independent, private, and stubborn.

Note: Do not get me wrong. I admired my parents' independence, stubbornness, and joie de vivre, their devil-may-care attitude. Looking back on those times, I now believe they used this as armor to avoid the discussions they knew were inevitable. This armor is precisely what I had to get through in the future legs of the journey. In my discussions about this book with people since my parents passed, I have come to believe that the kind of deflection my parents exhibited is common. In fact, I have found all their emotions and reactions matched the stories and examples I found as I researched end-of-life norms. So, do not be surprised if your loved ones exhibit similar patterns. From the statistics cited earlier, it is clear that many people believe they should be having these conversations, but just as clearly, they are not doing so. I believe my parents were the same way.

CHAPTER 3
TAXIING OUT

Mom and Dad approached the move to the retirement facility with their usual independence and directness. They decided which items were going to accompany them to the new location, which were going to be given to which child (whether we wanted them or not), and which were going to be given to charity or disposed of in another way. I helped where I could and tried not to admit I was going to miss having them right across the street.

The move went off without incident except when my parents went to the dining room of the new facility for the first time. Prior to this evening, they had stayed in their own apartment in the independent living portion of the facility or dined out or with friends who also lived at the facility. On this particular evening, they went to the communal dining room and came back quite shaken from the experience. That night, Mom called me and related their shock that the dining room did not serve alcohol. I believe Mom's exact words were "the damn place is dry!" I pointed out that the facility was affiliated with the Baptist church and that they might have known that, and included it in their calculus, had they spent a little time exploring *before* their decision to move. My castigation was not met with great enthusiasm.

Despite the various dry regions of the facility, which could easily be avoided, Mom and Dad settled in. Mom had an easier time fitting in than Dad, except for one small quirk. Mom had always been outgoing, and she threw herself into the task of getting to know her new surroundings and neighbors. The only fly in the ointment was Mom's sometimes colorful language. Many were the times in those early months that the director of the facility would call me and ask if I could talk to my mom about her rather salty speech. Apparently, her "g**-d***ing" this and that was not appreciated at the Baptist facility! Dad was always well-spoken but a little less enthusiastic about his new surroundings. He preferred cerebral activities to social activities anyway, and the increasing pain in his back made socializing seem rather tedious to him. I went by at least once or twice a week for lunch or a visit and continued to see them out at various events and parties.

It was during this period that I pushed for a broader, deeper discussion of how the current situation was going to end. I believe my exact words were, "How does this movie end?" At first, they did not understand the question. They said we had arranged for all the needed end-of-life medical and legal documents and discussed all funeral arrangements, so why keep asking? It was dawning on me that funeral planning and legal documents dealt with only the biological and rational parts of our lives. The emotional and biographical end-of-life discussions were weighing on me. How did my parents want the inevitable end to come? Where? Who did they want around, and what did they want to be said? All these questions swirled in my mind as I tried to get them to engage. One particular exchange sticks out in my mind. After asking again how the movie ended, they said they would go to bed one night and not wake up in the morning. I replied, "That's a great plan. How will you pull it off?" Not surprisingly, they had no answer.

They should have known my questioning would continue. When my parents named me executor (along with Alec), I told them it was good news and bad news. The good news was, I adored them and would do anything for them. The bad news was, I am a planner and a stickler for detail. As usual, they did not want to talk about these very personal but inevitable decisions. But I am persistent. I kept asking, and I kept telling my parents that we needed to talk about these things. As I persisted, it became a little game for us. We would exchange pleasantries, talk about other things, and soon after we settled in, either they would ask me when I was going to ask them, or I would chime in. At least they were now laughing about it and even initiating the discussion. Humor and openness were signs of progress to me. It takes time. This is not a race to be won or a process to be checked off efficiently. These discussions must be teased out over time with love and empathy.

As time went on, we settled into a rhythm of discussions when I hit upon an idea. The facility Mom and Dad were in was a progressive care center that had accommodations for all the end stages of life, except acute (hospital) care. Mom and Dad were in the independent living section of the facility, which basically provided apartment-style living with on-site access to all your typical needs: bank, hairdresser, barber, and tailor. A primary care doctor was on-site, and the facility offered transportation to specialists. Several eating options were available, as well as various hobby and group activities.

Transportation took the residents to stores, events, and local attractions.

The assisted living portion of the facility offered much greater access to medical care and assistance for those who needed it, in exchange for a slight intrusion on privacy and independence. The long-term and mental-care facilities were for residents who needed constant medical attention and assistance.

The idea struck me to take Mom and Dad on a guided tour of the advanced facilities. I knew they had not really paid attention to these facilities when they received their orientation. I announced that, upon my next visit, we were going to tour all the next stations where the train they had boarded was going to stop. I called the nursing director, who had become a friend, and told her of my wish. She heartily agreed, and we set a date.

The day of our tour came, and I drove over to my parents' place. Our first stop was the assisted living area. The hallways and rooms were bright and airy, meticulously clean, and neat. The residents' doors were open so that the staff could see them and have easy access. Each room was decorated with a few personal items to make the residents feel at home. Medical personnel and staff buzzed from the central monitoring station and flitted in and out of the residents' rooms. I had specifically timed this tour to coincide with a mealtime. All the residents were either seated at their designated spots at communal tables or being served in their rooms.

As my parents took in the scenes, I could see concern dawning on their faces. We poked around a bit more and then ducked into a small conference room. "What do you think?" I asked. Both of my parents paused. "Are the doors always open?" my mom asked. "Yes," said the nursing director. "We need to be able to see if the residents are OK. We also have monitors in the rooms that connect to the central monitoring station." My dad asked, "Do we have to eat in the communal area?" The answer was "yes" unless special arrangements were made to eat in one's room or with family outside of the assisted living area.

The director was justifiably proud of the amenities and care. Everyone we met was kind and gracious. A sense of nurture and care was palpable. As a child, I was comforted knowing my parents would be well monitored and cared for. My parents, however, were appalled, as I knew they would be. Here, for all to see, were the intrusion and dependence they so vigorously hoped to avoid.

I gathered my parents and the nursing director, and we continued our tour. The next stop was the long-term care facility. Here again, the facility was immaculate, with a visible step up in the intensity and ubiquity of medical monitoring equipment. The facility and care were not what shocked my parents. What visibly unnerved them was the state of the residents. Many were incoherent and almost lifeless, unable to exist without care and assistance. It did not take long before both of my parents asked to end the tour.

I thanked the director, and we walked back to Mom and Dad's apartment in silence. When we arrived, my parents got busy around the apartment. I finally corralled them and asked again, "What do you think?" Mom was the first to answer: "Never put us in either of those facilities!" I pointed out that the whole experience was designed to end up there. I added that the care was terrific and that we, as their children, would feel comfortable with them being there. They said that was not the issue. Neither could fathom ending their lives in such a place, surrounded by and dependent upon strangers—kind, caring professionals—but strangers none-the-less. I said, "Well, then, you had better start talking to me about what you *do* want."

The tour had the intended effect. Mom and Dad now saw gaps in their plans, and we discussed them in earnest. These were still not comfortable discussions, and Mom and Dad did not easily undertake them, but with love and persistence, we uncovered the biographical and emotional stories we all needed to share.

My informal talks in the ten years since these events confirm that this resistance is not unusual. Doctors, caregivers, and family members have all told me they faced the same suit of armor with these discussions. But it is not just the parents who struggle with these discussions. Just recently, I met with a woman about the subject of this book, and she implored me to get it out as soon as possible. She was trying to talk with her children about her wishes, and they were the ones deflecting. These are not easy discussions for anyone to have but have them you should.

CHAPTER 4
SORRY, THERE ARE NO DIRECT FLIGHTS

*We shall not cease from exploration,
and the end of all our exploring
will be to arrive where we started
and know the place for the first time.*
— T. S. Eliot

A s I suspected, the original plan of going to sleep one night and not waking up did not work, and life pleasantly bumbled along for my parents, generally uneventful. However, Dad's back pain continued to worsen, and he became even less mobile and interested in socializing. Due to the many surgeries and scar tissue on his back, he was unable to feel a particularly bad abrasion that developed from sitting and exercising in a recumbent bike. Unbeknownst to any of us, due to Dad's stoicism and Mom's dismissive, hands-off caregiving, this abrasion turned into a nasty open wound, a decubitus ulcer, commonly called a bed sore. Ulcers such as these are notoriously hard to manage, especially when they are in areas where blood flow is limited, and the pressure and abrasion continues. Doctors recommended changes in chairs, mattresses, sleeping positions, and diet, but all suggestions were met with the usual dismissive attitude and stoicism.

As my father progressed into his eighties, other age-related issues visited Dad as well. He grew increasingly incontinent and had trouble with his swallowing and eyesight. All these ailments were "manageable" with medication and therapy. As bad as his other ailments were, however, the worst specter for Dad was Alzheimer's. His mother had succumbed to early-onset Alzheimer's and was lost to the family for years, although she had continued to live.

She and Dad were among the first patients in a longitudinal study of Alzheimer's, and Dad knew he was at risk. For a cerebral man like my father, the prospect of losing his mind but not his life terrified him.

All the medical and age-related issues culminated in a general loss of dexterity, acuity, and interest in life. Our whole family felt Dad was depressed, and the doctor recommended anti-depressants, but Dad steadfastly refused, and Mom supported him. They both came from a generation and a philosophy that sneered at such notions. Their approach, as with everything, was to just grit your teeth and work through it.

Early on in this period, I had the occasion to ride with Dad as he drove his car. It was an eye-opening experience. We arrived back at the facility and went to the apartment. I sat down next to Dad and came right to the point: "Dad, driving is not going to work for you anymore!" He did not initially take well to this line of discussion. He allowed, "In my condition, I don't much care if I kill myself." I said, "That may well be true, but you are not who I am worried about. I am worried you will harm someone else!" It was clear he had not thought about it from that perspective. We parted on somewhat cool terms, but I told him I loved him and would see him in a few days. To his great credit, the next time we met, he pushed his keys across the table to me and said, "You're right. My driving is not particularly good, and I am a danger to myself and others." I like to think our regular discussions about the changes of this time in their lives informed and facilitated his decision.

Not long after Dad gave up driving, we were talking, and I asked him how he was doing. I was glad to hear he found he really did not miss it as much as he thought he would. Since he now had a front-row seat, I asked him, "How is Mom's driving?" His short response was, "Terrifying!" It was clear from this brief interlude that I had another driving talk in my near future.

About this time, a new threat to my parents' independence emerged. Dad's condition was declining to the point that he was at risk of not passing the test that determined his ability to remain in the independent living part of the facility. The ulcer in Dad's back was constantly getting infected, and consequently, he was repeatedly being put on antibiotics. Dad was vehemently opposed to assisted living; a position confirmed after several short stays in long-term care necessitated by short hospital stays or other medical issues. During a series of infections caused by the ulcer, he had stayed in a monitored bed in extended care after each episode to make sure he was able to move back to independent living.

The up-and-down journey wore on all of us and precipitated a series of discussions with the management of the facility. During one of Dad's routine visits to the primary care doctor at the facility, the doctor asked Dad how he was doing. Dad cynically replied, "If I still had my guns, I would just shoot myself." And with that, I was in the director's office discussing my father being placed on suicide watch.

I appreciated the facility's sensitivity to the topic and the internal alert system. I talked with Dad and Mom, and he assured me he was just joking. I pointed out that it was not a joking matter to the care providers at the facility and that they were required to report such events. We again discussed depression and possible treatments, but Dad steadfastly refused, claiming he was not depressed, just practical. Unfortunately, our discussions did not stop the references, and I received several more summonses to the director's office.

As we discussed Dad's declining physical condition, Mom and I decided that when the time came, we would bring care into the apartment so that Dad could stay where he was comfortable and not have to be separated from Mom. Even though they both understood the need for this step, I could still see their resentment at being dependent on others. Their dislike of the invasion of their privacy and concern about being a burden to anyone was readily apparent. The good news was, we were having the end-of-life discussions, even if they were hard and sometimes involved unpleasant topics.

It would be a lie to say these continuing discussions did not take their toll on me. Sometimes I resented the calls and the intrusions, but I resolved to complete the process with Mom and Dad. I knew they had done the same for me at the start of my life. It seemed almost fated and symmetrical that I should return the favor at the end of theirs. I believe if I had not pursued the discussions with my parents early on, we would have had an exceedingly difficult time having them under the extreme conditions that were arising.

CHAPTER 5
THE FIRST LEG OF THE JOURNEY: DAD'S FLIGHT

My father didn't tell me how to live; he lived and let me watch him do it.
— Clarence Budington Kelland

I was happily engaged in an activity with my family when the call came. It was the director: "We need to talk. Your dad has been put on suicide watch again." So, off I went. This was one of the times I was less than charitable about having taken on this supporting role in my parents' life. Mom, who was much more mobile, was out of town with an old friend.

Dad and I spoke openly and frankly. Frustrated, I said, "Dad, you have got to stop talking about killing yourself." We had a long

47

talk, and he admitted that he was miserable with his current life. He felt he had led a great life and did not want to live anymore with his medical conditions. He claimed he was not depressed, only tired of it all. I told him I knew that, and in fact, all of us knew it. I went further, "If you're serious, then let's talk about it. I will help you. I am all in for you." While I may have, in the moment, offered a variety of options ranging from practical to far-fetched, my message to my father was, "I know you are miserable but complaining and threatening are not helpful for any of us. You can either do something about it or live with it. Those are the choices."

"You'd do that for me?" he said.

"Absolutely, if that is what <u>you</u> want. I know you are hurting; I know you are scared; I know you don't want to go on, and I want to help. But you will have to talk to me—and to Mom and to all your children—about this decision and the actions you decide to take. Let's explore the options together. I will help you. I believe that the process of exploration will either confirm your decision or reverse it."

This was a break-through day. For me, it felt like I was finally getting through to the biographical and emotional essence of Dad's end-of-life flight plan. For Dad, I think it was a form of approval, of permission for me to explore such thoughts and not think ill of him or question his desires. That proved to be true.

I explored the literature and publicly available resources about the decision to end one's own life consciously, willingly. In some places in the world, these deliberations are legal and supported. I talked to doctors, nurses, and other health care providers. I contacted local hospice providers to learn about this option, a condition known in medical and hospice parlances as a failure to thrive. I talked to attorneys versed in end-of-life care and eventually shared all my findings, thoughts, and questions with Dad, and the family.

One of these forays led me to a retired internal medicine doctor who sympathized with my father's plight and his desires. During one of our talks, we explored the idea of Dad just stopping his medicines, speculating that a recurring infection would eventually accomplish the desired end. But this seemed like an agonizing route. As we explored further, the doctor recommended having Dad voluntarily stop eating as well as ceasing his medicines. He pointed out that eating is the activity that sustains all of us, but that it is a *choice* we all make. One could, therefore, make a choice not to eat, with the inevitable consequence of denying the body the nutrients needed to persist. Essentially, this retried doctor said it is the same as deciding in an advanced medical directive not to have a feeding tube inserted to supply essential nutrients. It struck me that this was the door Dad was looking for and would provide the control he was seeking. I passed along my findings to Mom and Dad. For the first time in a long time, I saw a glimmer of hope in my dad's face. We all had questions, but it felt like we were finally making progress.

I know that sounds like a terrible thing to say, but we all found hope, even if it was hope for a swift end. The certainty and control this option offered seemed infinitely better than his gnawing despair.

I traveled again to see the doctor who suggested this latest course of action. I asked about the timing: should it be gradual or abrupt? I asked about hydration. The doctor explained that if the body were hydrated, the denial of food would not be painful—aside from the expected hunger pangs, which could be managed with various techniques. Over a relatively short period of time, depending on underlying health conditions, the patient would become more and more lethargic, slip into a quiescent state, and finally succumb. The process would be accelerated if the infection came back as they had so often. He assured me that the process would be painless and manageable. We discussed the appropriate liquids to maintain proper hydration. Obviously, water was the least sustaining, and the quantity could be unlimited. Other liquids would be fine and would aid with hydration but would obviously extend the period, depending on the calorie count. Knowing my father's penchant for a cocktail or two, I asked rather snidely if alcohol was a liquid. "Last time I checked," the doctor replied with a wink.

Dad, Mom, and I continued our discussions, now focused on the idea of Dad voluntarily deciding to refuse his medications and stop eating. We concluded this was the certainty and the control he so desperately desired. I summarized our deliberations with my siblings to make sure they understood. After some questioning, they all agreed with the course of action. These were not easy discussions. They were emotional and sad, but we all knew it was what Dad wanted.

Being the planner I am, I wanted to make sure everyone was aware of Dad's intent. So, Dad dictated to me his final desires. I transcribed them and made sure Dad, Mom, Alec and all our siblings had access to the draft for sufficient time to raise any doubts or questions. Hearing none, I had Dad and Mom sign the statement, with Alec and I witnessing. We then set about advising everyone with a need to know what my father had decided.

To be absolutely sure of our standing, I arranged for our estate attorney to meet with Mom, Dad, and me. He had not been involved in this process and would, therefore, be a good gauge of response. I met him at the facility and told him of my father's wishes and shared with him Dad's statement. He then met with Mom alone to make sure she agreed and understood the consequences. Finally, we ushered him in to see Dad alone. After a considerable time, he emerged from the room and declared, "It is clear what his intentions are and that he is pre-pared for the eventuality." He assured us that Dad's affairs were in order and that nothing we were doing was contrary to any laws.

During these final weeks, Dad had suffered another episode with a hospital stay and was forced to stay in long-term care again upon his return. At this point, Dad qualified for hospice under a failure to thrive diagnosis from his conditions. As we prepared for moving back into the apartment and into hospice care, my siblings came to see Dad. I insisted that he personally tell each one of his decision. As a function of schedules, it turned out that my brother Colie was the last child to see Dad during this process. Colie had been a part of the deliberations and completely supported the decision, so there were no surprises. In fact, I will never forget the exchange. When Colie walked into the room, my father was visibly more relaxed. It was as if he had been counting off the members of his family with whom he had to have the discussion and gain permission. Colie came to Dad's bedside and asked how he was. Dad's reply was, "I just want to die!" "I know, Pop," Colie said, "and we're all OK with that!"

Dad moved back into the apartment and into the spare room, which had been set up with a hospital bed by the hospice provider. We got Dad settled in and began a wonderful series of visits to say goodbye. Since we were all aware of the circumstances and the decisions, the finality felt liberating. We laughed and cried and told tales. We rejoiced in Dad's life, and he relaxed, knowing he was once again in control.

Just as the doctor had predicted, Dad gradually declined in energy and became frail. Since he had abandoned all medicine except for the palliative care medications provided by hospice, it was only a matter of time before the infection or lack of nutrients, or both, took him. One night, close to the end, several of us were gathered at Mom and Dad's. We wheeled Dad out in a wheelchair so that he could see his family gathered for him. My sister Beirne poured a glass of champagne for him and placed it on the tray near him. He rather weakly asked, "What's that?" pointing to the champagne. Beirne said, "It's champagne." Dad grabbed the glass, raised it to all of us, and pronounced, "*Bon*."

During these final days, I noticed that Dad when he was awake, seemed concerned about something. I also noticed that Mom seemed to avoid being with him. I put two and two together and went in search of my mother. I sat her down and said, "Mom, you have to go in one last time and tell Dad you are OK with this. I believe he is waiting for you to say that, and I think you are avoiding it." To my mom's great credit, she agreed. Later that day, Mom went in to see Dad alone. Shortly thereafter, my dad died.

I believe my father was greatly comforted by finally being in control of and certain about his life and inevitable death. The calmness and serenity that enveloped him and my mother during this time spoke volumes about the power of having these important discussions.

Note: I recognize that the subject matter of this chapter could be triggering for some people. Just because my father chose this does not mean it is the right decision and course of action for everyone. We did all we could to make his choice safe and thoughtfully carried out with input from physicians and other medical and legal advisors. The decisions are not what are important here, it is the discussions that lead to the decisions that matter. The decisions are personal, and each person will have to make their own, but the discussions are shared and make all the difference in the end.

CHAPTER 6
THE SECOND LEG OF THE JOURNEY: MOM'S FLIGHT

Those we love don't go away;
they sit beside us every day.
— Liane Moriarty

Mom and Dad had been great dancers and taught all of us children to dance. Even still, our whole family loves to dance. Occasionally, after Dad died and Mom and I were visiting, I would dance with Mom at the apartment. The only music in their apartment was a CD of Frank Sinatra's greatest hits stuck in Dad's old laptop. The CD drive door would not open, so our only choice was Frank. Not bad and we made do. We were usually having a drink and listening to the CD; then Mom would ask me to dance. She was in her eighties, and of course frail, so we did not move a lot, but we had great fun. It seemed to connect us both to Dad.

The family continued to visit, and we would bounce from my house to Mom's apartment. Mom had a spare bedroom in the apartment and occasionally family members would stay with her. It was obvious that Mom was lonely and sad, but she continued to exhibit the stoic, stubborn resolve that marked her life. Always independent and hardheaded, she refused to wallow and retreat. Again, I had to admire her resolve and devil-may-care attitude, but they did bring certain concerns.

One night, after a wonderful dinner at Mom's favorite restaurant, Mom and my sister-in-law, Georgia, were returning to her apartment. It had snowed and the parking lot and sidewalks were slick. Stories vary, but whether it was the snowy conditions or an impromptu snowball fight, Mom who was never one to back down or give in to her frailty, apparently got a little too carried away on the walk in and fell, hitting her head on a curb, badly cutting, and bruising her forehead.

I got a call from Georgia that the facility had sent her by ambulance to the hospital and off I went to assess the damage. Mom acted as if nothing had happened, and it was all perfectly normal. The discharging doctor asked me if anyone was staying with my mom that night because they were worried about potential concussion symptoms and wanted someone to monitor her. I told him there was.

On the way back to the facility, Mom asked if I was mad at her for her behavior. How could I be mad at her for having fun in her eighties? I did tell her that I was worried about the blow to her head and any lingering effects, but I had to add, "As hardheaded as you are, the only real damage was probably to the curb!" Then I got serious. I told Mom that she needed to alert Georgia or pull the call strap in the apartment if she felt unusual or her headaches intensified. Mom asked why, and I told her the doctor was worried about her having an episode in the night. Mom said, in classic fashion, "Oh, hell, I don't need anyone to babysit me!" I allowed that was probably true and that I knew she was not worried, adding, "Perhaps you are planning to act out the whole 'we are just going to go to bed one night and not wake up' plan, huh?"

"It wouldn't hurt my feelings," was her predictable reply. She too was ready.

On another occasion, I got a call from the facility saying my mom was being seen in the clinic for possible dehydration. I went to the facility where I learned the circumstances behind the clinic visit. Mom had driven to the grocery store in our neighborhood, close to where she and Dad had lived. Talk about a creature of habit; she had never switched to the same-brand store closer to the facility. Her truck would not start, and rather than calling me or my wife, she had decided to walk back to the facility with her groceries, some four and a half miles away.

Apparently, she had become overheated and disoriented on a major thoroughfare. Fortunately, a kind man saw her and inquired. He gave her a ride to the facility and stayed with her until she was attended to. After the event, we were relaxing in the apartment, and I asked her why she had not called me or anyone else. She simply replied, "I didn't want to bother you." She was stubborn, independent, and selfless, and while I appreciated those qualities, I also wanted to strangle her.

The event with the groceries and the declining reliability of Mom's truck, driving, and decision-making finally culminated in my asking her to give up driving. At first, she resisted, but shortly after, she relented and informed me she had donated her truck to a veteran's group.

I continued to visit her regularly. We discussed family and any issues she might have. Mom continued to read voraciously. The facility had a borrowing library, and Mom frequented it often, usually to donate books she had read. Occasionally, the flow went the other direction, and she would borrow a book for her own reading pleasure. It was on just such an occasion that Mom demonstrated her long-standing streak of stubborn independence and strong will. I noticed a rather ratty looking paperback that was clearly missing the cover and first pages by her chair. I inquired about the book and its condition, and my mom replied, "It's a crappy book." So, as she finished the pages, she just tore them off rather than preserve them since clearly no one else would want to read such tripe. Did I mention my mom was headstrong and independent?

We continued to include Mom at family events, with one of us picking her up. My siblings came to visit and would stay with Mom or with my wife and me. Many of these visits ended up at Mom's favorite restaurant. It was not far from her apartment, and the staff had come to know my mom and dad well. One waiter had struck up a friendship with Mom and was always gracious and welcoming to her and all of us. So much so, when he saw her name on the reservation list or saw her coming across the parking lot, he usually had a bourbon on the rocks waiting for her.

And so, it was one night when Alec and I took Mom to the restaurant. We arrived at the restaurant, and sure enough, a bourbon was waiting for my mom at the table. We had a delightful dinner, talking and laughing about family and friends. Alec asked Mom how she was doing, and she said she was fine. We both asked her how her health was and if she had anything, she wanted to share with us as her executors. She said no that we had said it all. She thanked Alec, me, and our siblings for having had the end-of-life discussions. Now, that was a switch from earlier times. She said she was lonely but prepared for whatever came next.

We had been seated near the door to the restaurant, and during our conversation, a mutual friend came through the door. Before we knew it, Mom was on her feet, greeting the acquaintance in her usual outgoing, boisterous manner. Whether it was the rapid movements, the close quarters, the Jack Daniels, or a combination this greeting did not go well. Mom toppled over backward, and her head banged hard on the floor from the momentum of the fall. Everyone close to the scene heard the sickening sound, and a small army gathered around to see if she was all right. All were concerned and questions flew: "What happened? Are you OK? Did you trip? Are you hurt?"

Mom calmly looked at the assembled crowd and announced, "I am fine. I just S-T-U-M-B-L-E-D," spelling out the word so that we all knew she was lucid. Reflecting on the prior doctor's concerns about concussive events, Alec and I debated staying with Mom that night. I knew she would not want either of us to do that, but I went anyway. She popped out of bed the next morning as if nothing had happened and told me it had not been necessary for me to have spent the night. She went on to say if she had experienced an episode in the night, she was fine with that too! Did I mention she was hardheaded?

So, things progressed: a laugh here, a stumble there. We continued to talk, reminisce, and dance. As I have related, my mom was never a very sentimental sort, and she had always had a habit of throwing things away and cleaning up. During one visit, she shared with me her contempt for the exceptionally large, old TV my dad had watched. The set was almost as big as she was and had now become public enemy number one for her. I knew that if I did not do anything, she would try to solve the problem herself. I left that day with specific instructions to her not to try to move the TV herself. I told her I would be back the next day to move it. You probably already know where this is going.

Late the same afternoon I received a call from the facility that Mom, complaining of her back hurting, had been transported to the hospital. When I got to the emergency room, Mom was clearly in extreme pain and discomfort. I asked her what had happened and was upset, but not surprised, to find she had tried to pick up the TV herself. She reported feeling as if she had pulled something in her back. It turned out to be far worse. At her advanced age, Mom's bones were very brittle. When she went to pick up the TV, she cracked multiple vertebrae down her spine, like "unzipping a zipper" the doctor said. Unfortunately, nothing could be done for her except to immobilize the back, try to make her feel comfortable, and keep her from doing too much.

This last episode seemed to really deflate my mom. Ordinarily, she would power her way through pain and obstacles, but this injury seemed to go to her heart and essence, and she resented the medications and attention. She stayed in the long-term care part of the facility for her convalescence, but she could not get comfortable and had a hard time sleeping. In time, she became more mobile, was released from the long-term care center, and resumed some of her activities, but she was just not the same. I noticed she seemed confused and disoriented more often. We started talking more seriously about her end-of-life desires to make sure she was still resolute in them. As fate would have it, those discussions came to a head quickly.

CHAPTER 7
CLEARED FOR FINAL TAKEOFF

*Always let them think of you
as singing and dancing.*
— Anita Brookner

Not long after Mom returned to her apartment in independent living, I was out of town when I got a call from the facility. The staff had found her quite confused and thought I should come home and check on her. We drove home that night, and I planned to go the next morning. The next morning, before I could leave the house, the facility called and said one of the residents had seen her wandering the halls and that she was incoherent. The staff did not find her in her apartment when they searched. When I arrived at the facility, I ran in and almost immediately saw my mother slumped in a chair in the hall near her apartment, clearly in extremis. A staff member from the facility came from the other direction at about the same time. We gathered her up, got her to the apartment, and pulled the emergency call strap. Within minutes, a nurse from the clinic who knew Mom and I well came into the apartment. Mom was clearly having some sort of episode, and the nurse called for an ambulance. As Mom became more agitated, the nurse and I tried to calm her down. Soon the EMTs arrived, assessed Mom, sedated her, and packed her onto a gurney. Off we went to the hospital.

I spent a long and trying day in the emergency room as Mom was seen and tested. Mom was clearly hallucinating because she kept referring to a window just out of reach. She repeatedly asked me to open the window she saw on her right, even though we were in a windowless treatment room. Late in the day, she was moved to a room in the hospital, and we waited for news of her condition. Mom was asleep, sedated, or both when an internist from the hospital came to tell me the news. Mom had suffered a cerebellar stroke. He indicated we would know more in the morning after the in-charge doctor examined her and reviewed all the test results, but he warned considerable impairment should be expected. I called my siblings in tears and informed them of Mom's status.

The next day, as we were waiting for the various doctors, I noted some of the impairments. Mom complained of having blurred or compromised vision on her left side. She clearly had trouble speaking normally, and her left side seemed weak. Finally, late in the afternoon, a hospital internist came and thoroughly examined Mom. When he was done, he motioned me to the side of the bed and explained to Mom what had happened and her condition. He could not have been kinder and gentler, but he was direct.

"Mrs. Donaldson, you have suffered a rather severe cerebellar stroke. We caught it in good time, but there is still some impairment. You have probably noticed that your left side is most affected. You will notice that your vision and acuity on the left side is blocked or blurry. This may impair your reading. Your mouth and tongue probably feel different on that side, too. You may experience some minor trouble speaking, chewing, and swallowing. Similarly, your left arm, leg, and whole left side will seem sluggish and unresponsive. All these conditions can be very well managed with physical and speech therapy. Your heart, lungs, and all of your vital signs are great for a woman of your age, and as I said, the lingering symptoms of the stroke can all be managed with therapy."

As the doctor explained her condition, I watched Mom carefully. She did not flinch or blink or show any emotion. I knew exactly what she was thinking. I knew my mother could not and would not be the person the doctor was describing. I had sensed that, as the doctor recited the litany of issues brought on by the stroke, my mom was envisioning her plane ticket out.

"Mrs. Donaldson, would you like me to provide orders for the various therapies to start immediately?"

"No," was her one-word response.

"All of the conditions the doctor mentioned are manageable, Mom," I added, knowing she would not agree to any of the therapies.

"I know," she said.

The doctor and I waited for her response.

"What would you like, Mrs. Donaldson?" the doctor asked.

"I want to return to my home, enter hospice, and live out my last days, just like my husband did." I explained to the doctor that we had gone through a similar process with my dad and that we, as a family, were prepared for such an eventuality. I told him we had all discussed these end-of-life matters and were all certain of Mom's wishes. The doctor made a note on Mom's chart, gave an order sheet to the nurse, and asked Mom if she had any more questions.

My mom perked up and asked, "Can I have my bourbon now?"

The doctor smiled and said, "Unfortunately, I cannot prescribe bourbon for you in the hospital, Mrs. Donaldson." Upon hearing this, Mom put her head back on the pillow and pronounced, "Oh, s**t!" Unfiltered right to the end.

On the way out of the room, the doctor motioned me to walk with him. As we entered the hallway, he said, "Your Mom is quite a woman. Get her some bourbon and tell her I said to enjoy it." I thanked him for his kindness and warm bedside manner, and then he did something interesting. He thanked me and my siblings for preparing so well for our parents' end-of-life decisions. He mentioned that, too often, it is left up to him and his partners and the nurses to force hard conversations during stressful times. He said it was refreshing to see a family that had dealt with these issues in advance.

Mom settled back into the facility in the same room in their apartment where Dad had been. She had stipulated the same conditions as Dad, no medicines other than palliative and no food. Hospice came and set up a hospital bed. Once again, the family took turns visiting Mom and saying our long goodbyes. Again, these times were electric with sadness and laughter and love. During one visit Alec, Beirne, and I were taking turns visiting with Mom, all together at her apartment early one evening. The hospice nurse was bathing Mom, and we were talking and reminiscing, reliving past stories of Mom and Dad. The nurse left, and it was my turn to take Mom her bourbon. We all made ourselves a drink, and I took Mom's and mine into her room. I sat on the bed near her and gave her the drink. We touched glasses, and she unexpectedly said, "I wish we could still dance."

"So do I, Mom. That would be great fun."

"Well, we could sing!" she replied. Now, that was not technically true. Neither of us could sing a lick. But we would try.

"What shall we sing, your favorite, *Dancing in the Dark*?" I inquired.

"No, not that one." She paused several moments and said, "Let's sing *Dancing Cheek to Cheek*." We clinked glasses and sang softly. Mom was weak and we both forgot the lyrics and just hummed in places. I know I cried. The love and fondness between us were palpable. Some six hours later, she had died.

She knew! I am convinced she knew her time was at hand. The lyrics to the classic Sinatra tune which she did not want to sing are all about facing an ending together. I think she knew that and still wanted to somehow protect me from the inevitable even though we had talked about it so openly for so long. Right then, singing *Dancing Cheek to Cheek* gave her a connection to Dad, me, and to her past life, but she knew that life was ending.

As sad as this evening was, one could not ask for a better ending: knowing you are going to die yet being totally prepared; singing lovingly with your child, even though neither of you can sing; and remembering the wonderful times you had. Wouldn't it be great if we all could experience such an exit?

CHAPTER 8
CLEARING CUSTOMS:
ANYTHING TO DECLARE?

Death is not the greatest loss in life. The greatest loss is what dies inside us while we live.
— Norman Cousins

What I learned in shepherding my parents on these journeys is that end-of-life discussions, while hard and sad, are also incredibly liberating and rewarding. The certainty and feeling of control these conversations brought proved comforting since, one way or another, I would inevitably lose my parents. Fearing this eventual end is not only stupid but it also gets in the way of enjoying the time you do have with your loved ones. So, do not wait until after the trip. Do not miss the opportunity to take control of this event. Have the discussions you need to have. Make these declarations ahead of time in your flight plan. You can do it.

Here are some final thoughts:

- **Do not wait**: Since death is inevitable, why not talk about what you think and feel about that inevitability? If you are a parent, open up to your children about your wishes and thoughts. If they do not want to talk, write out your ideas and mail them. Ask to talk after they have read them. If you are a child of older parents, press your parents for their thoughts and desires. Tell them it is important for you to know those thoughts and desires so you can be prepared to carry them out and be ready for what is to come.

- **Talk early**: Dealing with these discussions at the last minute, during highly stressful episodes, does not help matters at all. As morbid as it sounds, the best time to have these discussions is when you feel the most alive. Being reasonably sure the specter of death is some time off relieves some of the stress the topic inevitably brings.

- **Talk often**: People can change their minds and uncover new philosophies, so do not feel pressured to talk once and resolve all the issues on the first pass.

- **Write it down**: Whatever decisions you come to, as parent or child, write them down. Make sure they are clear and exactly what the other party—or parties—intended.

- **Share it**: Share these thoughts with everyone who needs to know.

I hope my experience of shepherding my parents to the end will give you courage and inspire you to make a flight plan for your journey. Bon voyage!

POSTFACE

The doctor's comment to me about how well we prepared our parents and ourselves for the inevitable end of life really highlighted the need for this book. These are not preparations doctors, nurses, caregivers, lawyers, and insurance executives can or should undertake. Only parents, sons, daughters, and loved ones can have these discussions. Trust me when I tell you, I know they are hard and emotional, but have them you should. You might be asking, "But do they help?" I found that they did. I believe having these discussions and the certainty they brought to all my family helped soften the grief profile. While my parents' deaths were undeniably sad and filled with grief, there was no regret about what was left unsaid, no wondering what could have been.

So, is there evidence to support having end-of-life (EOL) discussions such as I describe as being helpful? Dr. Sherman Lee, a colleague and psychology professor who specializes in grief research, shared his findings with me and I pass them along to you.

Is there evidence to support EOL discussions?

Yes, EOL discussions do help. In a Journal of the American Medical Association study, EOL discussions were found to be associated with less aggressive medical care near death and earlier hospice referrals. (Wright et al., 2008).

Why is this finding important?

Most patients prefer to end their lives this way. For example, 80% of older adult patients with a serious illness, surveyed in a Canadian hospital, prefer a less aggressive and more comfort-oriented end-of life care plan that does not include CPR. Studies also suggest that patients with cancer wish to be involved in making decisions regarding their medical care at the end of life. (as cited in You et al., 2014).

Do EOL discussions cause psychological harm to the patients?

No. Despite some physicians' concerns, EOL discussions were not found to be associated with increased emotional distress or psychiatric disorders among these patients. (Wright et al., 2008).

What should be covered during EOL discussions?

5 elements are important to address (You et al., 2014):

- Preferences for care in the event of a life-threatening illness.
- Values.
- Prognosis.
- Fears or Concerns.
- Questions about goals of care.

What are the benefits of covering these 5 elements in EOL discussions?

Research demonstrated that addressing more elements was associated with (You et al., 2014):

- Greater concordance between patients' preferences and prescribed goals of care.
- Greater patient satisfaction.

Are there ways to improve EOL discussions?

Yes, include video. In a randomized controlled trial study of patients with cancer, the results showed that patients who viewed a 6-minute video presenting the three levels of medical care were (You et al., 2014):

- More likely to prefer comfort measures.
- More likely to avoid CPR.
- More knowledgeable regarding the subject matter.

- More certain of their decision when compared to patients only hearing a verbal narrative.

I believe the video described above acts as a proxy for the kind of discussions I have been describing herein. I would encourage you to have these discussions in person and not rely on a disembodied video. Don't miss the opportunity for the certainty and comfort you will gain through having them.

CONCLUSIONS

The proceeding is the story of my parents' decisions, decisions they made because of our frank and open discussions. I do not mean to imply they are the only decisions one can make. You, gentle reader will have to make your own decisions based on your desires and beliefs. You might be asking, "So, where are you on this topic?" As you might imagine, I have thought a lot about it. Here is where I have ended up as of the writing of this book.

I don't fear the act of dying. How can I? It is inevitable. To say I fear death is akin to saying I fear breathing, eating, or feeling my heart pumping—all inevitable functions and consequences of life. However, I have a few qualifying statements:

- I fear dying without having a say in how that happens and having a plan to make it sensible and manageable for all.
- I fear not having the courage to talk about my wishes and make clear my intentions.
- I fear being a burden on my family and friends.
- I fear dying alone in the company of strangers who never knew me or my wishes.
- I fear bankrupting my family with medical costs from preserving a life that is not worth living.

If I can control the above, I do not have to fear death. My death is inevitable. I can only fear being ill-prepared and not preparing my family and friends for the inevitable. But how can I be unprepared for the inevitable? Only by being obdurate and selfish, and I don't want to be either of those during my life.

FINAL THOUGHTS

r. Jacob Appel in his illuminating book, *Who Says You're Dead*, poses the very serious question of who decides your end-of-life conditions. He basically asks the reader to ponder who they want making their end-of-life decisions for them.

Many will look at my parents' choices to accelerate the end their life in the manner of their choosing and declare it suicide, and they may be uncomfortable with the idea that I helped them with that choice. Merriam Webster defines suicide as "the act or an instance of taking one's own life voluntarily and intentionally." If we take that definition literally, then that is what I did. But here's the thing, and this is where the rational and biological and emotional and biographical stories collide. My parents advanced medical directives instructed us to not use feeding tubes and artificial means to extend life. That is the biological and rational part of the flight plan. By consciously choosing to cease eating and deny their bodies of nutrients, my parents were making the biographic and emotional equivalents of those decisions. That was their flight plan, the one they controlled. I believe that level of control made all the difference in their end-of-life planning.

Since death is inevitable, the very act of being born starts the process of taking one's life, because you cannot not die. So, we all intend to die at some point. The differences in how we view this term lie in the connotation of the word and our intentionality. I propose, as does Dr. Appel, the intentionality is in reflecting on one's life and sharing your intentions with those you love and who love you. That is vastly different than the intentionality of the tragic connotation of suicide, where people in pain retreat from the world and their loved ones. To make this distinction clear, I have started using a new word to highlight the difference.

Idecide is the act of informing your loved ones, friends, family, and others close to you of your intention to be in control of your life's end. See what I just did there? Idecide: I decide. I decide on my end-of-life—not my doctors, my diseases, my family members, my caregivers, or my insurance company. Idecide!

As I said earlier, death is not the opposite of life; it is the opposite of birth. Life is what we do in between those two polar events.

> *The day which we fear as our last is*
> *but the birthday of eternity.*
> — Seneca the Younger

ABOUT THE AUTHOR

Willy is an educator, author, businessman, systems thinker, husband, father, friend, and son who likes to think deeply and longitudinally about ideas big and small.

He is the author of *Simple Complexity: A Management Book for the Rest of Us: A Guide to Systems Thinking.*

ABOUT THE PICTURE

This is my favorite picture of my parents. It was taken as they emerged from the church on their wedding day. In working with my friend and brilliant photographer, Jesse Hutcheson, we happened to catch my image reflecting on their picture. It seemed like a perfect image for this book.

NOTES

1   https://en.wikipedia.org/wiki/Flight_plan
2   https://www.aarp.org/money/investing/
    info-2017/half-of-adults-do-not-have-
    wills.html
3   https://www.reuters.com/article/
    us-health-usa-advance-directives/over-
    one-third-of-u-s-adults-have-advanced-
    medical-directives-idUSKBN19W2NO
4   Source: The Conversation Project
    National Survey (2018),
    https://theconversationproject.org/
5   Survey of Californians by the California
    HealthCare Foundation (2012),
    https://www.chcf.org/

A free ebook edition is available with the purchase of this book.

To claim your free ebook edition:

1. Visit MorganJamesBOGO.com
2. Sign your name CLEARLY in the space
3. Complete the form and submit a photo of the entire copyright page
4. You or your friend can download the ebook to your preferred device

Morgan James
BOGO™

A FREE ebook edition is available for you
or a friend with the purchase of this print book.

CLEARLY SIGN YOUR NAME ABOVE

Instructions to claim your free ebook edition:
1. Visit MorganJamesBOGO.com
2. Sign your name CLEARLY in the space above
3. Complete the form and submit a photo of this entire page
4. You or your friend can download the ebook to your preferred device

Print & Digital Together Forever.

Snap a photo

Free ebook

Read anywhere

Printed in the USA
CPSIA information can be obtained
at www.ICGtesting.com
JSHW082359140824
68134JS00020B/2165